Let's talk about mental health.

---

this journal belongs to:

_____   _____
NAME   PHONE NUMBER

_____
EMAIL

_____
HOME ADDRESS

You are enough

MENTAL HEALTH TOOLKIT

PURPOSE

This journal was created to help you take charge of your mental health and well-being. Journaling is an effective way for you to manage stress, anxiety, depression, and other mental health challenges. It's a safe space to express your emotions, reflect on your thoughts, and track your progress.

Whether you're new to journaling or have been doing it for years, this journal is a valuable tool for you to have in your mental health toolkit. Regular journaling is a proactive step toward maintaining good mental health.

You. Got. This.

IT'S OK TO ASK FOR HELP.

ASKING FOR HELP

CIRCLE OF SUPPORT

If you're feeling overwhelmed, don't hesitate to ask for some extra help! Your loved ones can be a great source of support & help connect you with a professional you can talk to. You could also try joining a group or talking to someone at work or school.

Just remember, you don't have to go through tough times alone!

my support system

_____   _____
NAME   PHONE NUMBER

_____
EMAIL

_____   _____
NAME   PHONE NUMBER

_____
EMAIL

_____   _____
NAME   PHONE NUMBER

_____
EMAIL

_____   _____
NAME   PHONE NUMBER

_____
EMAIL

Please note: Our journals are not meant to cure, treat or prevent any medical or mental health conditions and the information within the pages of this journal should not be used as a replacement for professional advice.

TIPS & TRICKS

GETTING STARTED

There is no wrong way to journal, but developing the habit takes practice. Try these tips to help you make journaling a part of your daily routine.

✓ **pick a time**
Choose a time in your daily routine to journal. Many people prefer to journal in the morning or before bed to help them ease into or out of their day.

✓ **keep it simple**
Start simple; write out your day & how were feeling, include the details. This can help you get used to putting your thoughts on paper. Even just writing out a to-do list for the next day can help you fall asleep faster.

✓ **speak your truth**
To get the most out of journaling, be honest with yourself. Write down your thoughts and feelings without holding back. This can be difficult, but it's important to be vulnerable and not water down your thoughts.

✓ **get cozy**
Find a private space to write in where you feel comfortable & safe. Maybe a cozy corner in your home or a spot in your office that's just for you. Get comfortable with a soft blanket, warm socks, or a cup of tea!

✓ **ask for help**
If your thoughts and feelings become too overwhelming, consider talking to a trusted loved one or seeking professional help from a therapist. Reach out to your circle of support!

RESOURCES

INSIDE YOUR JOURNAL

Within the pages of this journal, you will find a range of prompts designed to guide you toward better mental health. From self-reflection and gratitude prompts to mindfulness exercises and self-care check-in pages, each section is crafted to help you cultivate a positive mindset, enhance your self-awareness, & foster a sense of purpose.

mental health check-in pages
- These pages are dedicated to tracking mental health progress
- They provide a space to write down symptoms, mood changes, & overall well being

writing prompts
- Provides valuable insight into managing your emotions & responses to different situations
    - **Gratitude:** Focuses on the positive aspects of life & appreciation of good things
    - **Mindfulness:** Helps focus on the present moment & awareness of thoughts, feelings, & actions
    - **Self-Reflection:** Gain insight into your thoughts, feelings, & behaviors
    - **Positive Thinking:** Encourages examination of your actions & reactions to make positive changes

coloring pages
- Provides a relaxing activity & stress-relief
- Enhances creativity & focus

blank lined journal pages
- Encourages daily reflection & personal growth
- Provides space for goal-setting, note-taking, and brainstorming

Deep breaths. You got this.

RATE YOUR OVERALL WELLNESS
😊 🙂 😯 😠 😢 😐 😑

DATE _____

M T **W** T **F** S **S**

WATER
💧 💧 💧 💧 💧 💧 💧 💧

MY SLEEP LAST NIGHT WAS...
😍 Great 🙂 Good 😐 Okay 😟 Not good 😣 Awful

gratitude
What am I grateful for today?

self-reflect
Actions, reactions & positive change.

What do I need to take care of myself today?
_____
_____
_____
_____

What have I learned about myself lately?
_____
_____
_____
_____

mindfulness
What thoughts & emotions have been on my mind?

How can I be kinder to myself today?
_____
_____
_____
_____
_____
_____
_____

self-care
Are you finding balance?

Think about each of the life categories to the right.

Rate each category from 1 - 10.

(Wheel of life: PERSONAL GROWTH, HEALTH, FRIENDS, RELATIONSHIPS, RECREATION, SPIRITUALITY, CAREER, FINANCE — rated 1-10)

self-aware
How am I today?

○ Happy ○ Frustrated
○ Sad ○ Anxious
○ Content ○ Tired
○ Overwhelmed ○ Bored
○ Insecure ○ Sick
○ Excited ○ Angry
○ Lonely ○ Emotionless
○ _____

RATE YOUR OVERALL WELLNESS

☺ ☹ 😯 😠 😢 😐 😶

DATE _____

[M] T [W] T [F] s [S]

WATER
○ ○ ○ ○ ○ ○ ○ ○

MY SLEEP LAST NIGHT WAS...
☺ Great ☺ Good 😐 Okay ☹ Not good 😢 Awful

gratitude
What am I grateful for today?

self-reflect
Actions, reactions & positive change.

What do I need to take care of myself today?
_____
_____
_____
_____

What have I learned about myself lately?
_____
_____
_____
_____
_____

How can I be kinder to myself today?
_____
_____
_____
_____
_____
_____

mindfulness
What thoughts & emotions have been on my mind?

self-care
Are you finding balance?

Think about each of the life categories to the right.

Rate each category from 1 - 10.

Wheel of life chart with categories: PERSONAL GROWTH, HEALTH, FRIENDS, RELATIONSHIPS, RECREATION, SPIRITUALITY, CAREER, FINANCE. Scale 1-10.

self-aware
How am I today?

○ Happy   ○ Frustrated
○ Sad   ○ Anxious
○ Content   ○ Tired
○ Overwhelmed   ○ Bored
○ Insecure   ○ Sick
○ Excited   ○ Angry
○ Lonely   ○ Emotionless
○ _____

RATE YOUR OVERALL WELLNESS

DATE _____

M T W T F S S

WATER
◊ ◊ ◊ ◊ ◊ ◊ ◊ ◊ ◊ ◊

MY SLEEP LAST NIGHT WAS...
Great Good Okay Not good Awful

gratitude
What am I grateful for today?

self-reflect
Actions, reactions & positive change.

What do I need to take care of myself today?
_____
_____
_____
_____

What have I learned about myself lately?
_____
_____
_____
_____

mindfulness
What thoughts & emotions have been on my mind?

How can I be kinder to myself today?
_____
_____
_____
_____
_____
_____
_____

self-care
Are you finding balance?

Think about each of the life categories to the right.

Rate each category from 1 - 10.

PERSONAL GROWTH · HEALTH · FRIENDS · RELATIONSHIPS · RECREATION · SPIRITUALITY · CAREER · FINANCE

self-aware
How am I today?

○ Happy   ○ Frustrated
○ Sad   ○ Anxious
○ Content   ○ Tired
○ Overwhelmed   ○ Bored
○ Insecure   ○ Sick
○ Excited   ○ Angry
○ Lonely   ○ Emotionless
○ _____

RATE YOUR OVERALL WELLNESS	DATE _____
😊 🙂 😮 😠 😢 😶 😐	M T W T F S S

WATER
💧 💧 💧 💧 💧 💧 💧 💧

MY SLEEP LAST NIGHT WAS...
😍 Great 🙂 Good 😕 Okay 😟 Not good 😣 Awful

gratitude
What am I grateful for today?

self-reflect
Actions, reactions & positive change.

What do I need to take care of myself today?
_____
_____
_____

What have I learned about myself lately?
_____
_____
_____

mindfulness
What thoughts & emotions have been on my mind?

How can I be kinder to myself today?
_____
_____
_____
_____
_____

self-care
Are you finding balance?

Think about each of the life categories to the right.

Rate each category from 1 - 10.

Wheel with categories: PERSONAL GROWTH, HEALTH, FRIENDS, RELATIONSHIPS, RECREATION, SPIRITUALITY, CAREER, FINANCE (scale 1-10)

self-aware
How am I today?

○ Happy   ○ Frustrated
○ Sad   ○ Anxious
○ Content   ○ Tired
○ Overwhelmed   ○ Bored
○ Insecure   ○ Sick
○ Excited   ○ Angry
○ Lonely   ○ Emotionless
○ _____

RATE YOUR OVERALL WELLNESS

😊 🙂 😐 🙁 😢 😶 😑

DATE _____

M T **W** T **F** S **S**

WATER
💧 💧 💧 💧 💧 💧 💧 💧

MY SLEEP LAST NIGHT WAS...
😍 Great 🙂 Good 😐 Okay 🙁 Not good 😫 Awful

gratitude
What am I grateful for today?

self-reflect
Actions, reactions & positive change.

What do I need to take care of myself today?
_____
_____
_____
_____

What have I learned about myself lately?
_____
_____
_____
_____

How can I be kinder to myself today?
_____
_____
_____
_____
_____
_____

mindfulness
What thoughts & emotions have been on my mind?

self-care

Are you finding balance?

Think about each of the life categories to the right.

Rate each category from 1 - 10.

PERSONAL GROWTH · HEALTH · FRIENDS · RELATIONSHIPS · RECREATION · SPIRITUALITY · CAREER · FINANCE

1 2 3 4 5 6 7 8 9 10

self-aware
How am I today?

○ Happy   ○ Frustrated
○ Sad   ○ Anxious
○ Content   ○ Tired
○ Overwhelmed   ○ Bored
○ Insecure   ○ Sick
○ Excited   ○ Angry
○ Lonely   ○ Emotionless
○ _____

RATE YOUR OVERALL WELLNESS

DATE _____

M T W T F S S

WATER
○ ○ ○ ○ ○ ○ ○ ○ ○

MY SLEEP LAST NIGHT WAS...
Great Good Okay Not good Awful

gratitude
What am I grateful for today?

self-reflect
Actions, reactions & positive change.

What do I need to take care of myself today?
_____
_____
_____
_____

What have I learned about myself lately?
_____
_____
_____
_____

mindfulness
What thoughts & emotions have been on my mind?

How can I be kinder to myself today?
_____
_____
_____
_____
_____
_____
_____

self-care
Are you finding balance?

Think about each of the life categories to the right.

Rate each category from 1 - 10.

PERSONAL GROWTH • HEALTH • FRIENDS • RELATIONSHIPS • RECREATION • SPIRITUALITY • CAREER • FINANCE

self-aware
How am I today?

○ Happy   ○ Frustrated
○ Sad   ○ Anxious
○ Content   ○ Tired
○ Overwhelmed   ○ Bored
○ Insecure   ○ Sick
○ Excited   ○ Angry
○ Lonely   ○ Emotionless
○ _____

RATE YOUR OVERALL WELLNESS

DATE _____

M T W T F S S

WATER
○ ○ ○ ○ ○ ○ ○ ○ ○ ○

MY SLEEP LAST NIGHT WAS...
Great Good Okay Not good Awful

gratitude
What am I grateful for today?

self-reflect
Actions, reactions & positive change.

What do I need to take care of myself today?
_____
_____
_____

What have I learned about myself lately?
_____
_____
_____
_____

How can I be kinder to myself today?
_____
_____
_____
_____
_____
_____

mindfulness
What thoughts & emotions have been on my mind?

self-care
Are you finding balance?

Think about each of the life categories to the right.

Rate each category from 1 - 10.

PERSONAL GROWTH · HEALTH · FRIENDS · RELATIONSHIPS · RECREATION · SPIRITUALITY · CAREER · FINANCE

self-aware
How am I today?

○ Happy   ○ Frustrated
○ Sad   ○ Anxious
○ Content   ○ Tired
○ Overwhelmed   ○ Bored
○ Insecure   ○ Sick
○ Excited   ○ Angry
○ Lonely   ○ Emotionless
○ _____

RATE YOUR OVERALL WELLNESS

DATE _____

M T W T F S S

WATER
○ ○ ○ ○ ○ ○ ○ ○

MY SLEEP LAST NIGHT WAS...
Great Good Okay Not good Awful

gratitude
What am I grateful for today?

mindfulness
What thoughts & emotions have been on my mind?

self-reflect
Actions, reactions & positive change.

What do I need to take care of myself today?
_____
_____
_____

What have I learned about myself lately?
_____
_____
_____
_____

How can I be kinder to myself today?
_____
_____
_____
_____
_____
_____

self-care
Are you finding balance?

Think about each of the life categories to the right.

Rate each category from 1 - 10.

PERSONAL GROWTH · HEALTH · FRIENDS · RELATIONSHIPS · RECREATION · SPIRITUALITY · CAREER · FINANCE

1 2 3 4 5 6 7 8 9 10

self-aware
How am I today?

○ Happy   ○ Frustrated
○ Sad   ○ Anxious
○ Content   ○ Tired
○ Overwhelmed   ○ Bored
○ Insecure   ○ Sick
○ Excited   ○ Angry
○ Lonely   ○ Emotionless
○ _____

RATE YOUR OVERALL WELLNESS

DATE _____

M T W T F S S

WATER
○ ○ ○ ○ ○ ○ ○ ○ ○ ○

MY SLEEP LAST NIGHT WAS...
Great Good Okay Not good Awful

gratitude
What am I grateful for today?

self-reflect
Actions, reactions & positive change.

What do I need to take care of myself today?
_____
_____
_____

What have I learned about myself lately?
_____
_____
_____

mindfulness
What thoughts & emotions have been on my mind?

How can I be kinder to myself today?
_____
_____
_____
_____
_____

self-care
Are you finding balance?

Think about each of the life categories to the right.

Rate each category from 1 - 10.

(Wheel of life: PERSONAL GROWTH, HEALTH, FRIENDS, RELATIONSHIPS, RECREATION, SPIRITUALITY, CAREER, FINANCE — scale 1-10)

self-aware
How am I today?

○ Happy   ○ Frustrated
○ Sad   ○ Anxious
○ Content   ○ Tired
○ Overwhelmed   ○ Bored
○ Insecure   ○ Sick
○ Excited   ○ Angry
○ Lonely   ○ Emotionless
○ _____

RATE YOUR OVERALL WELLNESS

😊 😐 😯 😣 😢 😬 😑

DATE _____

M T W T F s S

WATER
💧 💧 💧 💧 💧 💧 💧 💧

MY SLEEP LAST NIGHT WAS...
😍 Great 😊 Good 😕 Okay 😟 Not good 😫 Awful

gratitude
What am I grateful for today?

self-reflect
Actions, reactions & positive change.

What do I need to take care of myself today?
_____
_____
_____

What have I learned about myself lately?
_____
_____
_____

mindfulness
What thoughts & emotions have been on my mind?

How can I be kinder to myself today?
_____
_____
_____
_____
_____

self-care
Are you finding balance?

Think about each of the life categories to the right.

Rate each category from 1 - 10.

PERSONAL GROWTH · HEALTH · FRIENDS · RELATIONSHIPS · RECREATION · SPIRITUALITY · CAREER · FINANCE

self-aware
How am I today?

○ Happy   ○ Frustrated
○ Sad   ○ Anxious
○ Content   ○ Tired
○ Overwhelmed ○ Bored
○ Insecure   ○ Sick
○ Excited   ○ Angry
○ Lonely   ○ Emotionless
○ _____

RATE YOUR OVERALL WELLNESS

😊 😐 😮 😠 😢 😶 😐

DATE _____

M · T · W · T · F · S · S

WATER

💧 💧 💧 💧 💧 💧 💧 💧

MY SLEEP LAST NIGHT WAS...

😍 Great 🙂 Good 😐 Okay 😟 Not good 😣 Awful

---

gratitude
What am I grateful for today?

self-reflect
Actions, reactions & positive change.

What do I need to take care of myself today?
_____
_____
_____
_____

What have I learned about myself lately?
_____
_____
_____
_____

How can I be kinder to myself today?
_____
_____
_____
_____
_____
_____

mindfulness
What thoughts & emotions have been on my mind?

---

self-care

Are you finding balance?

Think about each of the life categories to the right.

Rate each category from 1 - 10.

Wheel of life categories: PERSONAL GROWTH, HEALTH, FRIENDS, RELATIONSHIPS, RECREATION, SPIRITUALITY, CAREER, FINANCE (scale 1-10)

self-aware
How am I today?

- ○ Happy
- ○ Sad
- ○ Content
- ○ Overwhelmed
- ○ Insecure
- ○ Excited
- ○ Lonely
- ○ _____

- ○ Frustrated
- ○ Anxious
- ○ Tired
- ○ Bored
- ○ Sick
- ○ Angry
- ○ Emotionless

RATE YOUR OVERALL WELLNESS

DATE _____

M T W T F S S

WATER
○ ○ ○ ○ ○ ○ ○ ○ ○ ○

MY SLEEP LAST NIGHT WAS...
Great Good Okay Not good Awful

gratitude
What am I grateful for today?

self-reflect
Actions, reactions & positive change.

What do I need to take care of myself today?
_____
_____
_____
_____

What have I learned about myself lately?
_____
_____
_____
_____
_____

mindfulness
What thoughts & emotions have been on my mind?

How can I be kinder to myself today?
_____
_____
_____
_____
_____
_____
_____
_____

self-care

Are you finding balance?

Think about each of the life categories to the right.

Rate each category from 1 - 10.

PERSONAL GROWTH · HEALTH · FRIENDS · RELATIONSHIPS · RECREATION · SPIRITUALITY · CAREER · FINANCE

1 2 3 4 5 6 7 8 9 10

self-aware
How am I today?

○ Happy   ○ Frustrated
○ Sad   ○ Anxious
○ Content   ○ Tired
○ Overwhelmed   ○ Bored
○ Insecure   ○ Sick
○ Excited   ○ Angry
○ Lonely   ○ Emotionless
○ _____

RATE YOUR OVERALL WELLNESS
😊 🙂 😐 😠 😢 😶 😑

DATE _____
M T **W** T **F** S **S**

WATER
💧 💧 💧 💧 💧 💧 💧 💧 💧 💧

MY SLEEP LAST NIGHT WAS...
😍 Great 🙂 Good 😐 Okay 😟 Not good 😵 Awful

gratitude
What am I grateful for today?

self-reflect
Actions, reactions & positive change.

What do I need to take care of myself today?
_____
_____
_____

What have I learned about myself lately?
_____
_____
_____

mindfulness
What thoughts & emotions have been on my mind?

How can I be kinder to myself today?
_____
_____
_____
_____
_____

self-care
Are you finding balance?

Think about each of the life categories to the right.

Rate each category from 1 - 10.

Wheel of life: PERSONAL GROWTH, HEALTH, FRIENDS, RELATIONSHIPS, RECREATION, SPIRITUALITY, CAREER, FINANCE — scale 1-10

self-aware
How am I today?

○ Happy   ○ Frustrated
○ Sad   ○ Anxious
○ Content   ○ Tired
○ Overwhelmed   ○ Bored
○ Insecure   ○ Sick
○ Excited   ○ Angry
○ Lonely   ○ Emotionless
○ _____

RATE YOUR OVERALL WELLNESS
😊 😕 😯 😠 😢 😷 😐

DATE _____

M T **W** T **F** s **S**

WATER
💧 💧 💧 💧 💧 💧 💧 💧

MY SLEEP LAST NIGHT WAS...
😍 Great 😊 Good 😐 Okay 😟 Not good 😩 Awful

gratitude
What am I grateful for today?

self-reflect
Actions, reactions & positive change.

What do I need to take care of myself today?
_____
_____
_____

What have I learned about myself lately?
_____
_____
_____
_____

mindfulness
What thoughts & emotions have been on my mind?

How can I be kinder to myself today?
_____
_____
_____
_____
_____
_____

self-care
Are you finding balance?

Think about each of the life categories to the right.

Rate each category from 1 - 10.

Wheel with categories: PERSONAL GROWTH, HEALTH, FRIENDS, RELATIONSHIPS, RECREATION, SPIRITUALITY, CAREER, FINANCE. Scale 1-10.

self-aware
How am I today?

○ Happy   ○ Frustrated
○ Sad   ○ Anxious
○ Content   ○ Tired
○ Overwhelmed   ○ Bored
○ Insecure   ○ Sick
○ Excited   ○ Angry
○ Lonely   ○ Emotionless
○ _____

RATE YOUR OVERALL WELLNESS	DATE
😊 🙂 😐 😠 😢 😶 😑	M T W T F S S

WATER
○ ○ ○ ○ ○ ○ ○ ○ ○ ○

MY SLEEP LAST NIGHT WAS...
😍 Great 🙂 Good 😐 Okay 😟 Not good 😢 Awful

gratitude
What am I grateful for today?

self-reflect
Actions, reactions & positive change.

What do I need to take care of myself today?
_____
_____
_____
_____

What have I learned about myself lately?
_____
_____
_____
_____

mindfulness
What thoughts & emotions have been on my mind?

How can I be kinder to myself today?
_____
_____
_____
_____
_____
_____

self-care
Are you finding balance?

Think about each of the life categories to the right.

Rate each category from 1 - 10.

Wheel of life with categories: PERSONAL GROWTH, HEALTH, FRIENDS, RELATIONSHIPS, RECREATION, SPIRITUALITY, CAREER, FINANCE — scale 1 to 10

self-aware
How am I today?

○ Happy   ○ Frustrated
○ Sad   ○ Anxious
○ Content   ○ Tired
○ Overwhelmed ○ Bored
○ Insecure   ○ Sick
○ Excited   ○ Angry
○ Lonely   ○ Emotionless
○ _____

RATE YOUR OVERALL WELLNESS	DATE _____
😊 😌 😳 😠 😢 🤐 😐	M T W T F S S

WATER
○ ○ ○ ○ ○ ○ ○ ○

MY SLEEP LAST NIGHT WAS...
😍 Great 😊 Good 😐 Okay 😟 Not good 😣 Awful

gratitude
What am I grateful for today?

self-reflect
Actions, reactions & positive change.

What do I need to take care of myself today?
_____
_____
_____

What have I learned about myself lately?
_____
_____
_____

mindfulness
What thoughts & emotions have been on my mind?

How can I be kinder to myself today?
_____
_____
_____
_____
_____
_____

self-care
Are you finding balance?

Think about each of the life categories to the right.

Rate each category from 1 - 10.

Wheel of life with categories: PERSONAL GROWTH, HEALTH, FRIENDS, RELATIONSHIPS, RECREATION, SPIRITUALITY, CAREER, FINANCE (scale 1-10)

self-aware
How am I today?

○ Happy   ○ Frustrated
○ Sad   ○ Anxious
○ Content   ○ Tired
○ Overwhelmed   ○ Bored
○ Insecure   ○ Sick
○ Excited   ○ Angry
○ Lonely   ○ Emotionless
○ _____

RATE YOUR OVERALL WELLNESS

DATE _____

M T W T F S S

WATER
◊ ◊ ◊ ◊ ◊ ◊ ◊ ◊ ◊ ◊

MY SLEEP LAST NIGHT WAS...
Great Good Okay Not good Awful

gratitude
What am I grateful for today?

self-reflect
Actions, reactions & positive change.

What do I need to take care of myself today?
_____
_____
_____

What have I learned about myself lately?
_____
_____
_____
_____

How can I be kinder to myself today?
_____
_____
_____
_____
_____
_____

mindfulness
What thoughts & emotions have been on my mind?

self-care
Are you finding balance?

Think about each of the life categories to the right.

Rate each category from 1 - 10.

PERSONAL GROWTH · HEALTH · FRIENDS · RELATIONSHIPS · RECREATION · SPIRITUALITY · CAREER · FINANCE

1 2 3 4 5 6 7 8 9 10

self-aware
How am I today?

○ Happy   ○ Frustrated
○ Sad   ○ Anxious
○ Content   ○ Tired
○ Overwhelmed   ○ Bored
○ Insecure   ○ Sick
○ Excited   ○ Angry
○ Lonely   ○ Emotionless
○ _____

get outside.
reach out to a friend.
drink some water.
get some sleep!
pet a dog.
exercise.
listen to music.

RATE YOUR OVERALL WELLNESS

😊 😌 😐 😠 😢 😶 😑

DATE _____

M T **W** T **F** S **S**

WATER
💧 💧 💧 💧 💧 💧 💧 💧

MY SLEEP LAST NIGHT WAS...
😍 Great 🙂 Good 😐 Okay 😟 Not good 😩 Awful

gratitude
What am I grateful for today?

self-reflect
Actions, reactions & positive change.

What do I need to take care of myself today?
_____
_____
_____
_____

What have I learned about myself lately?
_____
_____
_____
_____

mindfulness
What thoughts & emotions have been on my mind?

How can I be kinder to myself today?
_____
_____
_____
_____
_____
_____
_____

self-care

Are you finding balance?

Think about each of the life categories to the right.

Rate each category from 1 - 10.

(Wheel: PERSONAL GROWTH, HEALTH, FRIENDS, RELATIONSHIPS, RECREATION, SPIRITUALITY, CAREER, FINANCE — scale 1-10)

self-aware
How am I today?

○ Happy   ○ Frustrated
○ Sad   ○ Anxious
○ Content   ○ Tired
○ Overwhelmed ○ Bored
○ Insecure   ○ Sick
○ Excited   ○ Angry
○ Lonely   ○ Emotionless
○ _____

RATE YOUR OVERALL WELLNESS

😊 😐 😮 😠 😢 😷 😑

DATE _____

M T W T F S S

WATER
◊ ◊ ◊ ◊ ◊ ◊ ◊ ◊

MY SLEEP LAST NIGHT WAS...
😊 Great 🙂 Good 😕 Okay 😣 Not good 😫 Awful

gratitude
What am I grateful for today?

self-reflect
Actions, reactions & positive change.

What do I need to take care of myself today?
_____
_____
_____
_____

What have I learned about myself lately?
_____
_____
_____
_____

mindfulness
What thoughts & emotions have been on my mind?

How can I be kinder to myself today?
_____
_____
_____
_____
_____
_____
_____

self-care

Are you finding balance?

Think about each of the life categories to the right.

Rate each category from 1 - 10.

Wheel of life: PERSONAL GROWTH, HEALTH, FRIENDS, RELATIONSHIPS, RECREATION, SPIRITUALITY, CAREER, FINANCE — 1 to 10 scale

self-aware
How am I today?

○ Happy   ○ Frustrated
○ Sad   ○ Anxious
○ Content   ○ Tired
○ Overwhelmed   ○ Bored
○ Insecure   ○ Sick
○ Excited   ○ Angry
○ Lonely   ○ Emotionless
○ _____

RATE YOUR OVERALL WELLNESS

😊 😐 😯 😠 😢 😶 😑

DATE _____

M T **W** T **F** S **S**

WATER
💧 💧 💧 💧 💧 💧 💧 💧

MY SLEEP LAST NIGHT WAS...
😍 Great 😊 Good 😐 Okay 😞 Not good 😫 Awful

gratitude
What am I grateful for today?

self-reflect
Actions, reactions & positive change.

What do I need to take care of myself today?
_____
_____
_____

What have I learned about myself lately?
_____
_____
_____

mindfulness
What thoughts & emotions have been on my mind?

How can I be kinder to myself today?
_____
_____
_____
_____
_____

self-care

Are you finding balance?

Think about each of the life categories to the right.

Rate each category from 1 - 10.

PERSONAL GROWTH · HEALTH · FRIENDS · RELATIONSHIPS · RECREATION · SPIRITUALITY · CAREER · FINANCE

self-aware
How am I today?

○ Happy   ○ Frustrated
○ Sad   ○ Anxious
○ Content   ○ Tired
○ Overwhelmed   ○ Bored
○ Insecure   ○ Sick
○ Excited   ○ Angry
○ Lonely   ○ Emotionless
○ _____

RATE YOUR OVERALL WELLNESS

DATE _____

M T W T F S S

WATER
○ ○ ○ ○ ○ ○ ○ ○

MY SLEEP LAST NIGHT WAS...
Great Good Okay Not good Awful

gratitude
What am I grateful for today?

self-reflect
Actions, reactions & positive change.

What do I need to take care of myself today?
_____
_____
_____
_____

What have I learned about myself lately?
_____
_____
_____
_____

How can I be kinder to myself today?
_____
_____
_____
_____
_____
_____

mindfulness
What thoughts & emotions have been on my mind?

self-care
Are you finding balance?

Think about each of the life categories to the right.

Rate each category from 1 - 10.

PERSONAL GROWTH · HEALTH · FRIENDS · RELATIONSHIPS · RECREATION · SPIRITUALITY · CAREER · FINANCE

1 2 3 4 5 6 7 8 9 10

self-aware
How am I today?

○ Happy   ○ Frustrated
○ Sad   ○ Anxious
○ Content   ○ Tired
○ Overwhelmed   ○ Bored
○ Insecure   ○ Sick
○ Excited   ○ Angry
○ Lonely   ○ Emotionless
○ _____

RATE YOUR OVERALL WELLNESS	DATE
😊 🙂 😮 🙁 😢 😐 🙂	**M** T **W** T **F** S **S**

WATER 💧💧💧💧💧💧💧💧

MY SLEEP LAST NIGHT WAS...
😍 Great 🙂 Good 😐 Okay 🙁 Not good 😢 Awful

gratitude
What am I grateful for today?

self-reflect
Actions, reactions & positive change.

What do I need to take care of myself today?
_____
_____
_____

What have I learned about myself lately?
_____
_____
_____
_____

How can I be kinder to myself today?
_____
_____
_____
_____
_____
_____

mindfulness
What thoughts & emotions have been on my mind?

self-care
Are you finding balance?

Think about each of the life categories to the right.

Rate each category from 1 - 10.

Wheel of life: PERSONAL GROWTH, HEALTH, FRIENDS, RELATIONSHIPS, RECREATION, SPIRITUALITY, CAREER, FINANCE — rated 1-10

self-aware
How am I today?

○ Happy   ○ Frustrated
○ Sad   ○ Anxious
○ Content   ○ Tired
○ Overwhelmed ○ Bored
○ Insecure   ○ Sick
○ Excited   ○ Angry
○ Lonely   ○ Emotionless
○ _____

RATE YOUR OVERALL WELLNESS

DATE _____

M T W T F S S

WATER
○ ○ ○ ○ ○ ○ ○ ○ ○ ○

MY SLEEP LAST NIGHT WAS...
Great Good Okay Not good Awful

gratitude
What am I grateful for today?

mindfulness
What thoughts & emotions have been on my mind?

self-reflect
Actions, reactions & positive change.

What do I need to take care of myself today?
_____
_____
_____

What have I learned about myself lately?
_____
_____
_____
_____
_____

How can I be kinder to myself today?
_____
_____
_____
_____
_____
_____
_____

self-care

Are you finding balance?

Think about each of the life categories to the right.

Rate each category from 1 - 10.

PERSONAL GROWTH · HEALTH · FRIENDS · RELATIONSHIPS · RECREATION · SPIRITUALITY · CAREER · FINANCE

self-aware
How am I today?

○ Happy   ○ Frustrated
○ Sad   ○ Anxious
○ Content   ○ Tired
○ Overwhelmed   ○ Bored
○ Insecure   ○ Sick
○ Excited   ○ Angry
○ Lonely   ○ Emotionless
○ _____

RATE YOUR OVERALL WELLNESS

DATE _____

M T W T F S S

WATER
○ ○ ○ ○ ○ ○ ○ ○ ○ ○

MY SLEEP LAST NIGHT WAS...
Great   Good   Okay   Not good   Awful

gratitude
What am I grateful for today?

self-reflect
Actions, reactions & positive change.

What do I need to take care of myself today?
_____
_____
_____

What have I learned about myself lately?
_____
_____
_____

How can I be kinder to myself today?
_____
_____
_____
_____
_____

mindfulness
What thoughts & emotions have been on my mind?

self-care
Are you finding balance?

Think about each of the life categories to the right.

Rate each category from 1 - 10.

PERSONAL GROWTH · HEALTH · FRIENDS · RELATIONSHIPS · RECREATION · SPIRITUALITY · CAREER · FINANCE

self-aware
How am I today?

○ Happy   ○ Frustrated
○ Sad   ○ Anxious
○ Content   ○ Tired
○ Overwhelmed   ○ Bored
○ Insecure   ○ Sick
○ Excited   ○ Angry
○ Lonely   ○ Emotionless
○ _____

RATE YOUR OVERALL WELLNESS

DATE _____

M T W T F S S

WATER
◊ ◊ ◊ ◊ ◊ ◊ ◊ ◊

MY SLEEP LAST NIGHT WAS...
Great Good Okay Not good Awful

gratitude
What am I grateful for today?

self-reflect
Actions, reactions & positive change.

What do I need to take care of myself today?
_____
_____
_____

What have I learned about myself lately?
_____
_____
_____

mindfulness
What thoughts & emotions have been on my mind?

How can I be kinder to myself today?
_____
_____
_____
_____
_____

self-care
Are you finding balance?

Think about each of the life categories to the right.

Rate each category from 1 - 10.

Wheel categories: PERSONAL GROWTH, HEALTH, FRIENDS, RELATIONSHIPS, RECREATION, SPIRITUALITY, CAREER, FINANCE

self-aware
How am I today?

○ Happy   ○ Frustrated
○ Sad   ○ Anxious
○ Content   ○ Tired
○ Overwhelmed   ○ Bored
○ Insecure   ○ Sick
○ Excited   ○ Angry
○ Lonely   ○ Emotionless
○ _____

RATE YOUR OVERALL WELLNESS

DATE _____

M T **W** T **F** S **S**

WATER
○ ○ ○ ○ ○ ○ ○ ○ ○ ○

MY SLEEP LAST NIGHT WAS...
😍 Great 😊 Good 😐 Okay 😟 Not good 😣 Awful

gratitude
What am I grateful for today?

self-reflect
Actions, reactions & positive change.

What do I need to take care of myself today?
_____
_____
_____

What have I learned about myself lately?
_____
_____
_____
_____

How can I be kinder to myself today?
_____
_____
_____
_____
_____
_____

mindfulness
What thoughts & emotions have been on my mind?

self-care

Are you finding balance?

Think about each of the life categories to the right.

Rate each category from 1 - 10.

Wheel categories: PERSONAL GROWTH, HEALTH, FRIENDS, RELATIONSHIPS, RECREATION, SPIRITUALITY, CAREER, FINANCE (scale 1-10)

self-aware
How am I today?

○ Happy   ○ Frustrated
○ Sad   ○ Anxious
○ Content   ○ Tired
○ Overwhelmed ○ Bored
○ Insecure   ○ Sick
○ Excited   ○ Angry
○ Lonely   ○ Emotionless
○ _____

RATE YOUR OVERALL WELLNESS

DATE _____

M T **W** T **F** S **S**

WATER
○ ○ ○ ○ ○ ○ ○ ○

MY SLEEP LAST NIGHT WAS...
Great Good Okay Not good Awful

gratitude
What am I grateful for today?

self-reflect
Actions, reactions & positive change.

What do I need to take care of myself today?
_____
_____
_____

What have I learned about myself lately?
_____
_____
_____

mindfulness
What thoughts & emotions have been on my mind?

How can I be kinder to myself today?
_____
_____
_____
_____

self-care

Are you finding balance?

Think about each of the life categories to the right.

Rate each category from 1 - 10.

PERSONAL GROWTH · HEALTH · FRIENDS · RELATIONSHIPS · RECREATION · SPIRITUALITY · CAREER · FINANCE

1 2 3 4 5 6 7 8 9 10

self-aware
How am I today?

○ Happy   ○ Frustrated
○ Sad   ○ Anxious
○ Content   ○ Tired
○ Overwhelmed   ○ Bored
○ Insecure   ○ Sick
○ Excited   ○ Angry
○ Lonely   ○ Emotionless
○ _____

RATE YOUR OVERALL WELLNESS
☺ 😐 😯 😠 😢 😑 🙂

DATE _____

M T **W** T **F** S **S**

WATER
💧 💧 💧 💧 💧 💧 💧 💧

MY SLEEP LAST NIGHT WAS...
😍 Great ☺ Good 😐 Okay 😟 Not good 😢 Awful

gratitude
What am I grateful for today?

self-reflect
Actions, reactions & positive change.

What do I need to take care of myself today?
_____
_____
_____

What have I learned about myself lately?
_____
_____
_____

How can I be kinder to myself today?
_____
_____
_____
_____

mindfulness
What thoughts & emotions have been on my mind?

self-care
Are you finding balance?

Think about each of the life categories to the right.

Rate each category from 1 - 10.

Wheel categories: PERSONAL GROWTH, HEALTH, FRIENDS, RELATIONSHIPS, RECREATION, SPIRITUALITY, CAREER, FINANCE

self-aware
How am I today?

○ Happy   ○ Frustrated
○ Sad   ○ Anxious
○ Content   ○ Tired
○ Overwhelmed ○ Bored
○ Insecure   ○ Sick
○ Excited   ○ Angry
○ Lonely   ○ Emotionless
○ _____

RATE YOUR OVERALL WELLNESS

☺ 😐 😶 😠 😢 😬 😑

DATE _____

M T W T F S S

WATER

💧 💧 💧 💧 💧 💧 💧 💧

MY SLEEP LAST NIGHT WAS...
😍 Great 🙂 Good 😐 Okay 😟 Not good 😣 Awful

---

gratitude
What am I grateful for today?

self-reflect
Actions, reactions & positive change.

What do I need to take care of myself today?
_____
_____
_____

What have I learned about myself lately?
_____
_____
_____

mindfulness
What thoughts & emotions have been on my mind?

How can I be kinder to myself today?
_____
_____
_____
_____
_____

---

self-care

Are you finding balance?

Think about each of the life categories to the right.

Rate each category from 1 - 10.

Wheel categories: PERSONAL GROWTH, HEALTH, FRIENDS, RELATIONSHIPS, RECREATION, SPIRITUALITY, CAREER, FINANCE

self-aware
How am I today?

○ Happy   ○ Frustrated
○ Sad   ○ Anxious
○ Content   ○ Tired
○ Overwhelmed   ○ Bored
○ Insecure   ○ Sick
○ Excited   ○ Angry
○ Lonely   ○ Emotionless
○ _____

RATE YOUR OVERALL WELLNESS

DATE _____

M T **W** T **F** S **S**

WATER
○ ○ ○ ○ ○ ○ ○ ○ ○ ○

MY SLEEP LAST NIGHT WAS...
Great Good Okay Not good Awful

gratitude
What am I grateful for today?

self-reflect
Actions, reactions & positive change.

What do I need to take care of myself today?
_____
_____
_____
_____

What have I learned about myself lately?
_____
_____
_____
_____

mindfulness
What thoughts & emotions have been on my mind?

How can I be kinder to myself today?
_____
_____
_____
_____
_____
_____
_____

self-care

Are you finding balance?

Think about each of the life categories to the right.

Rate each category from 1 - 10.

PERSONAL GROWTH · HEALTH · FRIENDS · RELATIONSHIPS · RECREATION · SPIRITUALITY · CAREER · FINANCE

self-aware
How am I today?

○ Happy   ○ Frustrated
○ Sad   ○ Anxious
○ Content   ○ Tired
○ Overwhelmed   ○ Bored
○ Insecure   ○ Sick
○ Excited   ○ Angry
○ Lonely   ○ Emotionless
○ _____

RATE YOUR OVERALL WELLNESS

DATE _____

M T W T F S S

WATER
○ ○ ○ ○ ○ ○ ○ ○

MY SLEEP LAST NIGHT WAS...
Great Good Okay Not good Awful

gratitude
What am I grateful for today?

self-reflect
Actions, reactions & positive change.

What do I need to take care of myself today?
_____
_____
_____
_____

What have I learned about myself lately?
_____
_____
_____
_____

mindfulness
What thoughts & emotions have been on my mind?

How can I be kinder to myself today?
_____
_____
_____
_____
_____
_____
_____

self-care
Are you finding balance?

Think about each of the life categories to the right.

Rate each category from 1 - 10.

PERSONAL GROWTH • HEALTH • FRIENDS • RELATIONSHIPS • RECREATION • SPIRITUALITY • CAREER • FINANCE

1 2 3 4 5 6 7 8 9 10

self-aware
How am I today?

○ Happy   ○ Frustrated
○ Sad   ○ Anxious
○ Content   ○ Tired
○ Overwhelmed   ○ Bored
○ Insecure   ○ Sick
○ Excited   ○ Angry
○ Lonely   ○ Emotionless
○ _____

RATE YOUR OVERALL WELLNESS	DATE
😊 😐 😲 😠 😢 😶 😑	M T W T F S S

WATER
○ ○ ○ ○ ○ ○ ○ ○ ○ ○

MY SLEEP LAST NIGHT WAS...
😍 Great 🙂 Good 😐 Okay 😟 Not good 😫 Awful

gratitude
What am I grateful for today?

self-reflect
Actions, reactions & positive change.

What do I need to take care of myself today?
_____
_____
_____

What have I learned about myself lately?
_____
_____
_____
_____

How can I be kinder to myself today?
_____
_____
_____
_____
_____

mindfulness
What thoughts & emotions have been on my mind?

self-care
Are you finding balance?

Think about each of the life categories to the right.

Rate each category from 1 - 10.

Wheel of life: PERSONAL GROWTH, HEALTH, FRIENDS, RELATIONSHIPS, RECREATION, SPIRITUALITY, CAREER, FINANCE (1-10 scale)

self-aware
How am I today?

○ Happy   ○ Frustrated
○ Sad   ○ Anxious
○ Content   ○ Tired
○ Overwhelmed   ○ Bored
○ Insecure   ○ Sick
○ Excited   ○ Angry
○ Lonely   ○ Emotionless
○ _____

RATE YOUR OVERALL WELLNESS 😊 😐 😶 😠 😢 😶‍🌫️ 😑

DATE _____

M T W T F S S

WATER 💧 💧 💧 💧 💧 💧 💧 💧

MY SLEEP LAST NIGHT WAS...
😍 Great 🙂 Good 😐 Okay 🙁 Not good 😫 Awful

gratitude
What am I grateful for today?

self-reflect
Actions, reactions & positive change.

What do I need to take care of myself today?
_____
_____
_____

What have I learned about myself lately?
_____
_____
_____

mindfulness
What thoughts & emotions have been on my mind?

How can I be kinder to myself today?
_____
_____
_____
_____
_____

self-care
Are you finding balance?

Think about each of the life categories to the right.

Rate each category from 1 - 10.

PERSONAL GROWTH · HEALTH · FRIENDS · RELATIONSHIPS · RECREATION · SPIRITUALITY · CAREER · FINANCE

1 2 3 4 5 6 7 8 9 10

self-aware
How am I today?

○ Happy   ○ Frustrated
○ Sad   ○ Anxious
○ Content   ○ Tired
○ Overwhelmed ○ Bored
○ Insecure   ○ Sick
○ Excited   ○ Angry
○ Lonely   ○ Emotionless
○ _____

RATE YOUR OVERALL WELLNESS	DATE
😊 😌 😯 😠 😢 😎 🙂	**M** T **W** T **F** S **S**

WATER
💧 💧 💧 💧 💧 💧 💧 💧

MY SLEEP LAST NIGHT WAS...
😎 Great 🙂 Good 😐 Okay 🙁 Not good 😢 Awful

gratitude
What am I grateful for today?

self-reflect
Actions, reactions & positive change.

What do I need to take care of myself today?
_____
_____
_____

What have I learned about myself lately?
_____
_____
_____

mindfulness
What thoughts & emotions have been on my mind?

How can I be kinder to myself today?
_____
_____
_____
_____
_____

self-care
Are you finding balance?

Think about each of the life categories to the right.

Rate each category from 1 - 10.

[Wheel of life chart with categories: PERSONAL GROWTH, HEALTH, FRIENDS, RELATIONSHIPS, RECREATION, SPIRITUALITY, CAREER, FINANCE — scale 1-10]

self-aware
How am I today?

- ○ Happy
- ○ Sad
- ○ Content
- ○ Overwhelmed
- ○ Insecure
- ○ Excited
- ○ Lonely
- ○ _____

- ○ Frustrated
- ○ Anxious
- ○ Tired
- ○ Bored
- ○ Sick
- ○ Angry
- ○ Emotionless

RATE YOUR OVERALL WELLNESS 🙂 😐 😌 😠 😢 😊 😐

DATE _____

M T W T F S S

WATER 💧 💧 💧 💧 💧 💧 💧 💧

MY SLEEP LAST NIGHT WAS...
😍 Great 🙂 Good 😌 Okay 😟 Not good 😣 Awful

gratitude
What am I grateful for today?

self-reflect
Actions, reactions & positive change.

What do I need to take care of myself today?
_____
_____
_____
_____

What have I learned about myself lately?
_____
_____
_____
_____

mindfulness
What thoughts & emotions have been on my mind?

How can I be kinder to myself today?
_____
_____
_____
_____
_____
_____
_____

self-care

Are you finding balance?

Think about each of the life categories to the right.

Rate each category from 1 - 10.

Wheel categories: PERSONAL GROWTH, HEALTH, FRIENDS, RELATIONSHIPS, RECREATION, SPIRITUALITY, CAREER, FINANCE

self-aware
How am I today?

○ Happy   ○ Frustrated
○ Sad   ○ Anxious
○ Content   ○ Tired
○ Overwhelmed   ○ Bored
○ Insecure   ○ Sick
○ Excited   ○ Angry
○ Lonely   ○ Emotionless
○ _____

RATE YOUR OVERALL WELLNESS

😊 😐 😶 😠 😢 😐 😑

DATE _____

[M] T [W] T [F] S [S]

WATER
💧 💧 💧 💧 💧 💧 💧 💧 💧 💧

MY SLEEP LAST NIGHT WAS...
😍 Great 🙂 Good 😐 Okay 😕 Not good 😣 Awful

gratitude
What am I grateful for today?

self-reflect
Actions, reactions & positive change.

What do I need to take care of myself today?
_____
_____
_____

What have I learned about myself lately?
_____
_____
_____
_____

mindfulness
What thoughts & emotions have been on my mind?

How can I be kinder to myself today?
_____
_____
_____
_____
_____
_____
_____

self-care
Are you finding balance?

Think about each of the life categories to the right.

Rate each category from 1 - 10.

Wheel of life: PERSONAL GROWTH, HEALTH, FRIENDS, RELATIONSHIPS, RECREATION, SPIRITUALITY, CAREER, FINANCE (scale 1-10)

self-aware
How am I today?

○ Happy   ○ Frustrated
○ Sad   ○ Anxious
○ Content   ○ Tired
○ Overwhelmed   ○ Bored
○ Insecure   ○ Sick
○ Excited   ○ Angry
○ Lonely   ○ Emotionless
○ _____

RATE YOUR OVERALL WELLNESS

DATE _____

M T W T F S S

WATER
◊ ◊ ◊ ◊ ◊ ◊ ◊ ◊

MY SLEEP LAST NIGHT WAS...
Great Good Okay Not good Awful

gratitude
What am I grateful for today?

self-reflect
Actions, reactions & positive change.

What do I need to take care of myself today?
_____
_____
_____

What have I learned about myself lately?
_____
_____
_____
_____

mindfulness
What thoughts & emotions have been on my mind?

How can I be kinder to myself today?
_____
_____
_____
_____
_____
_____

self-care

Are you finding balance?

Think about each of the life categories to the right.

Rate each category from 1 - 10.

PERSONAL GROWTH · HEALTH · FRIENDS · RELATIONSHIPS · RECREATION · SPIRITUALITY · CAREER · FINANCE

1 2 3 4 5 6 7 8 9 10

self-aware
How am I today?

○ Happy   ○ Frustrated
○ Sad   ○ Anxious
○ Content   ○ Tired
○ Overwhelmed   ○ Bored
○ Insecure   ○ Sick
○ Excited   ○ Angry
○ Lonely   ○ Emotionless
○ _____

RATE YOUR OVERALL WELLNESS	DATE
🙂 🙂 😐 😠 ☹️ 😌 😑	M T W T F S S

WATER
💧 💧 💧 💧 💧 💧 💧 💧

MY SLEEP LAST NIGHT WAS...
😍 Great 🙂 Good 😐 Okay ☹️ Not good 😟 Awful

gratitude
What am I grateful for today?

self-reflect
Actions, reactions & positive change.

What do I need to take care of myself today?
_____
_____
_____
_____

What have I learned about myself lately?
_____
_____
_____
_____

mindfulness
What thoughts & emotions have been on my mind?

How can I be kinder to myself today?
_____
_____
_____
_____
_____
_____
_____

self-care
Are you finding balance?

Think about each of the life categories to the right.

Rate each category from 1 - 10.

PERSONAL GROWTH · HEALTH · FRIENDS · RELATIONSHIPS · RECREATION · SPIRITUALITY · CAREER · FINANCE

self-aware
How am I today?

○ Happy   ○ Frustrated
○ Sad   ○ Anxious
○ Content   ○ Tired
○ Overwhelmed   ○ Bored
○ Insecure   ○ Sick
○ Excited   ○ Angry
○ Lonely   ○ Emotionless
○ _____

RATE YOUR OVERALL WELLNESS 😊 🙂 😐 😟 😢 😁 😑

DATE _____

M T W T F S S

WATER
💧 💧 💧 💧 💧 💧 💧 💧

MY SLEEP LAST NIGHT WAS...
😍 Great 🙂 Good 😐 Okay 😟 Not good 😫 Awful

gratitude
What am I grateful for today?

self-reflect
Actions, reactions & positive change.

What do I need to take care of myself today?
_____
_____
_____

What have I learned about myself lately?
_____
_____
_____

mindfulness
What thoughts & emotions have been on my mind?

How can I be kinder to myself today?
_____
_____
_____
_____
_____

self-care
Are you finding balance?

Think about each of the life categories to the right.

Rate each category from 1 - 10.

PERSONAL GROWTH • HEALTH • FRIENDS • RELATIONSHIPS • RECREATION • SPIRITUALITY • CAREER • FINANCE

self-aware
How am I today?

○ Happy   ○ Frustrated
○ Sad   ○ Anxious
○ Content   ○ Tired
○ Overwhelmed   ○ Bored
○ Insecure   ○ Sick
○ Excited   ○ Angry
○ Lonely   ○ Emotionless
○ _____

RATE YOUR OVERALL WELLNESS

☺ ~ ・・ ☹ 😢 😐 😑

DATE _____

[M] T [W] T [F] S [S]

WATER
○ ○ ○ ○ ○ ○ ○ ○ ○

MY SLEEP LAST NIGHT WAS...
😍 Great ☺ Good 🙂 Okay 🙁 Not good 😢 Awful

gratitude
What am I grateful for today?

self-reflect
Actions, reactions & positive change.

What do I need to take care of myself today?
_____
_____
_____

What have I learned about myself lately?
_____
_____
_____

mindfulness
What thoughts & emotions have been on my mind?

How can I be kinder to myself today?
_____
_____
_____
_____
_____

self-care

Are you finding balance?

Think about each of the life categories to the right.

Rate each category from 1 - 10.

PERSONAL GROWTH · HEALTH · FRIENDS · RELATIONSHIPS · RECREATION · SPIRITUALITY · CAREER · FINANCE

self-aware
How am I today?

○ Happy   ○ Frustrated
○ Sad   ○ Anxious
○ Content   ○ Tired
○ Overwhelmed ○ Bored
○ Insecure   ○ Sick
○ Excited   ○ Angry
○ Lonely   ○ Emotionless
○ _____

RATE YOUR OVERALL WELLNESS

DATE _____

M T W T F S S

WATER
○ ○ ○ ○ ○ ○ ○ ○ ○ ○

MY SLEEP LAST NIGHT WAS...
Great Good Okay Not good Awful

gratitude
What am I grateful for today?

self-reflect
Actions, reactions & positive change.

What do I need to take care of myself today?
_____
_____
_____
_____

What have I learned about myself lately?
_____
_____
_____
_____

How can I be kinder to myself today?
_____
_____
_____
_____
_____
_____

mindfulness
What thoughts & emotions have been on my mind?

self-care
Are you finding balance?

Think about each of the life categories to the right.

Rate each category from 1 - 10.

PERSONAL GROWTH · HEALTH · FRIENDS · RELATIONSHIPS · RECREATION · SPIRITUALITY · CAREER · FINANCE

1 2 3 4 5 6 7 8 9 10

self-aware
How am I today?

○ Happy   ○ Frustrated
○ Sad   ○ Anxious
○ Content   ○ Tired
○ Overwhelmed   ○ Bored
○ Insecure   ○ Sick
○ Excited   ○ Angry
○ Lonely   ○ Emotionless
○ _____

RATE YOUR OVERALL WELLNESS

😊 😐 😳 😠 😢 😶 😕

DATE _____

| M | T | W | T | F | S | S |

WATER

💧 💧 💧 💧 💧 💧 💧 💧

MY SLEEP LAST NIGHT WAS...

😎 Great 🙂 Good 😌 Okay 😣 Not good 😫 Awful

gratitude
What am I grateful for today?

self-reflect
Actions, reactions & positive change.

What do I need to take care of myself today?
_____
_____
_____
_____

What have I learned about myself lately?
_____
_____
_____
_____

mindfulness
What thoughts & emotions have been on my mind?

How can I be kinder to myself today?
_____
_____
_____
_____
_____
_____
_____

self-care

Are you finding balance?

Think about each of the life categories to the right.

Rate each category from 1 - 10.

PERSONAL GROWTH · HEALTH · FRIENDS · RELATIONSHIPS · RECREATION · SPIRITUALITY · CAREER · FINANCE

1 2 3 4 5 6 7 8 9 10

self-aware
How am I today?

○ Happy   ○ Frustrated
○ Sad   ○ Anxious
○ Content   ○ Tired
○ Overwhelmed   ○ Bored
○ Insecure   ○ Sick
○ Excited   ○ Angry
○ Lonely   ○ Emotionless
○ _____

RATE YOUR OVERALL WELLNESS

DATE _____

M T W T F S S

WATER
○ ○ ○ ○ ○ ○ ○ ○

MY SLEEP LAST NIGHT WAS...
Great Good Okay Not good Awful

gratitude
What am I grateful for today?

self-reflect
Actions, reactions & positive change.

What do I need to take care of myself today?
_____
_____
_____
_____

What have I learned about myself lately?
_____
_____
_____
_____

mindfulness
What thoughts & emotions have been on my mind?

How can I be kinder to myself today?
_____
_____
_____
_____
_____
_____
_____
_____

self-care
Are you finding balance?

Think about each of the life categories to the right.

Rate each category from 1 - 10.

PERSONAL GROWTH · HEALTH · FRIENDS · RELATIONSHIPS · RECREATION · SPIRITUALITY · CAREER · FINANCE

1 2 3 4 5 6 7 8 9 10

self-aware
How am I today?

○ Happy   ○ Frustrated
○ Sad   ○ Anxious
○ Content   ○ Tired
○ Overwhelmed ○ Bored
○ Insecure   ○ Sick
○ Excited   ○ Angry
○ Lonely   ○ Emotionless
○ _____

RATE YOUR OVERALL WELLNESS

☺ ☺ ☺ ☹ ☹ 😐 😐

DATE _____

M T **W** T **F** s **S**

WATER
○ ○ ○ ○ ○ ○ ○ ○ ○ ○

MY SLEEP LAST NIGHT WAS...
😍 Great ☺ Good 😐 Okay ☹ Not good 😫 Awful

gratitude
What am I grateful for today?

self-reflect
Actions, reactions & positive change.

What do I need to take care of myself today?
_____
_____
_____

What have I learned about myself lately?
_____
_____
_____

mindfulness
What thoughts & emotions have been on my mind?

How can I be kinder to myself today?
_____
_____
_____
_____
_____

self-care
Are you finding balance?

Think about each of the life categories to the right.

Rate each category from 1 - 10.

Wheel: PERSONAL GROWTH, HEALTH, FRIENDS, RELATIONSHIPS, RECREATION, SPIRITUALITY, CAREER, FINANCE (scale 1-10)

self-aware
How am I today?

○ Happy   ○ Frustrated
○ Sad   ○ Anxious
○ Content   ○ Tired
○ Overwhelmed   ○ Bored
○ Insecure   ○ Sick
○ Excited   ○ Angry
○ Lonely   ○ Emotionless
○ _____

RATE YOUR OVERALL WELLNESS

DATE _____

M T W T F S S

WATER
○ ○ ○ ○ ○ ○ ○ ○

MY SLEEP LAST NIGHT WAS...
Great Good Okay Not good Awful

gratitude
What am I grateful for today?

self-reflect
Actions, reactions & positive change.

What do I need to take care of myself today?
_____
_____
_____
_____

What have I learned about myself lately?
_____
_____
_____
_____

mindfulness
What thoughts & emotions have been on my mind?

How can I be kinder to myself today?
_____
_____
_____
_____
_____
_____

self-care
Are you finding balance?

Think about each of the life categories to the right.

Rate each category from 1 - 10.

PERSONAL GROWTH · HEALTH · FRIENDS · RELATIONSHIPS · RECREATION · SPIRITUALITY · CAREER · FINANCE

1 2 3 4 5 6 7 8 9 10

self-aware
How am I today?

○ Happy   ○ Frustrated
○ Sad   ○ Anxious
○ Content   ○ Tired
○ Overwhelmed   ○ Bored
○ Insecure   ○ Sick
○ Excited   ○ Angry
○ Lonely   ○ Emotionless
○ _____

RATE YOUR OVERALL WELLNESS 😊 🙂 😐 😠 😢 😶 😐

DATE _____

M T W T F S S

WATER 💧 💧 💧 💧 💧 💧 💧 💧 💧 💧

MY SLEEP LAST NIGHT WAS...
😍 Great 🙂 Good 😐 Okay 😟 Not good 😩 Awful

gratitude
What am I grateful for today?

self-reflect
Actions, reactions & positive change.

What do I need to take care of myself today?
_____
_____
_____
_____

What have I learned about myself lately?
_____
_____
_____
_____

How can I be kinder to myself today?
_____
_____
_____
_____
_____
_____

mindfulness
What thoughts & emotions have been on my mind?

self-care
Are you finding balance?

Think about each of the life categories to the right.

Rate each category from 1 - 10.

Wheel of life: PERSONAL GROWTH, HEALTH, FRIENDS, RELATIONSHIPS, RECREATION, SPIRITUALITY, CAREER, FINANCE — rated 1 to 10

self-aware
How am I today?

○ Happy   ○ Frustrated
○ Sad   ○ Anxious
○ Content   ○ Tired
○ Overwhelmed ○ Bored
○ Insecure   ○ Sick
○ Excited   ○ Angry
○ Lonely   ○ Emotionless
○ _____

RATE YOUR OVERALL WELLNESS

DATE _____

M T W T F S S

WATER
○ ○ ○ ○ ○ ○ ○ ○

MY SLEEP LAST NIGHT WAS...
Great Good Okay Not good Awful

gratitude
What am I grateful for today?

self-reflect
Actions, reactions & positive change.

What do I need to take care of myself today?
_____
_____
_____

What have I learned about myself lately?
_____
_____
_____
_____

How can I be kinder to myself today?
_____
_____
_____
_____
_____

mindfulness
What thoughts & emotions have been on my mind?

self-care
Are you finding balance?

Think about each of the life categories to the right.

Rate each category from 1 - 10.

PERSONAL GROWTH · HEALTH · FRIENDS · RELATIONSHIPS · RECREATION · SPIRITUALITY · CAREER · FINANCE

1 2 3 4 5 6 7 8 9 10

self-aware
How am I today?

○ Happy   ○ Frustrated
○ Sad   ○ Anxious
○ Content   ○ Tired
○ Overwhelmed   ○ Bored
○ Insecure   ○ Sick
○ Excited   ○ Angry
○ Lonely   ○ Emotionless
○ _____

RATE YOUR OVERALL WELLNESS

😊 😐 😮 😠 😢 😶 😑

DATE _____

M T W T F S S

WATER
○ ○ ○ ○ ○ ○ ○ ○ ○ ○

MY SLEEP LAST NIGHT WAS...
😍 Great 😊 Good 😐 Okay 😟 Not good 😣 Awful

gratitude
What am I grateful for today?

self-reflect
Actions, reactions & positive change.

What do I need to take care of myself today?
_____
_____
_____

What have I learned about myself lately?
_____
_____
_____

How can I be kinder to myself today?
_____
_____
_____
_____
_____
_____

mindfulness
What thoughts & emotions have been on my mind?

self-care
Are you finding balance?

Think about each of the life categories to the right.

Rate each category from 1 - 10.

PERSONAL GROWTH · HEALTH · FRIENDS · RELATIONSHIPS · RECREATION · SPIRITUALITY · CAREER · FINANCE

self-aware
How am I today?

○ Happy   ○ Frustrated
○ Sad   ○ Anxious
○ Content   ○ Tired
○ Overwhelmed ○ Bored
○ Insecure   ○ Sick
○ Excited   ○ Angry
○ Lonely   ○ Emotionless
○ _____

RATE YOUR OVERALL WELLNESS	DATE
😊 😐 😌 😣 😢 😶 😑	M T W T F S S

WATER ○○○○○○○○○○

MY SLEEP LAST NIGHT WAS... Great / Good / Okay / Not good / Awful

gratitude
What am I grateful for today?

mindfulness
What thoughts & emotions have been on my mind?

self-reflect
Actions, reactions & positive change.

What do I need to take care of myself today?
_____
_____
_____

What have I learned about myself lately?
_____
_____
_____

How can I be kinder to myself today?
_____
_____
_____
_____
_____

self-care
Are you finding balance?

Think about each of the life categories to the right.

Rate each category from 1 - 10.

PERSONAL GROWTH / HEALTH / FRIENDS / RELATIONSHIPS / RECREATION / SPIRITUALITY / CAREER / FINANCE

1 2 3 4 5 6 7 8 9 10

self-aware
How am I today?

○ Happy ○ Frustrated
○ Sad ○ Anxious
○ Content ○ Tired
○ Overwhelmed ○ Bored
○ Insecure ○ Sick
○ Excited ○ Angry
○ Lonely ○ Emotionless
○ _____

RATE YOUR OVERALL WELLNESS	DATE
😊 😐 😮 😠 😓 😶 😑	M T W T F S S

WATER	MY SLEEP LAST NIGHT WAS...
💧💧💧💧💧💧💧💧💧💧	😍 Great 😊 Good 😐 Okay 😟 Not good 😣 Awful

gratitude
What am I grateful for today?

self-reflect
Actions, reactions & positive change.

What do I need to take care of myself today?
_____
_____
_____
_____

What have I learned about myself lately?
_____
_____
_____
_____

mindfulness
What thoughts & emotions have been on my mind?

How can I be kinder to myself today?
_____
_____
_____
_____
_____
_____
_____

self-care
Are you finding balance?

Think about each of the life categories to the right.

Rate each category from 1 - 10.

(Wheel of life: PERSONAL GROWTH, HEALTH, FRIENDS, RELATIONSHIPS, RECREATION, SPIRITUALITY, CAREER, FINANCE — scale 1-10)

self-aware
How am I today?

- ○ Happy
- ○ Sad
- ○ Content
- ○ Overwhelmed
- ○ Insecure
- ○ Excited
- ○ Lonely
- ○ _____

- ○ Frustrated
- ○ Anxious
- ○ Tired
- ○ Bored
- ○ Sick
- ○ Angry
- ○ Emotionless

RATE YOUR OVERALL WELLNESS

DATE _____

M T W T F S S

WATER
○ ○ ○ ○ ○ ○ ○ ○ ○ ○

MY SLEEP LAST NIGHT WAS...
Great Good Okay Not good Awful

gratitude
What am I grateful for today?

mindfulness
What thoughts & emotions have been on my mind?

self-reflect
Actions, reactions & positive change.

What do I need to take care of myself today?
_____
_____
_____

What have I learned about myself lately?
_____
_____
_____
_____

How can I be kinder to myself today?
_____
_____
_____
_____
_____
_____
_____

self-care
Are you finding balance?

Think about each of the life categories to the right.

Rate each category from 1 - 10.

PERSONAL GROWTH HEALTH
FINANCE FRIENDS
CAREER RELATIONSHIPS
SPIRITUALITY RECREATION

self-aware
How am I today?

○ Happy   ○ Frustrated
○ Sad   ○ Anxious
○ Content   ○ Tired
○ Overwhelmed   ○ Bored
○ Insecure   ○ Sick
○ Excited   ○ Angry
○ Lonely   ○ Emotionless
○ _____

RATE YOUR OVERALL WELLNESS	DATE
😊 😐 😮 ☹️ 😢 😶 😑	M T W T F S S

WATER ○ ○ ○ ○ ○ ○ ○ ○

MY SLEEP LAST NIGHT WAS...
😊 Great 🙂 Good 😐 Okay 😟 Not good 😢 Awful

gratitude
What am I grateful for today?

self-reflect
Actions, reactions & positive change.

What do I need to take care of myself today?
_____
_____
_____

What have I learned about myself lately?
_____
_____
_____

mindfulness
What thoughts & emotions have been on my mind?

How can I be kinder to myself today?
_____
_____
_____
_____
_____

self-care

Are you finding balance?

Think about each of the life categories to the right.

Rate each category from 1 - 10.

Wheel of life categories: PERSONAL GROWTH, HEALTH, FRIENDS, RELATIONSHIPS, RECREATION, SPIRITUALITY, CAREER, FINANCE — scaled 1-10

self-aware
How am I today?

○ Happy   ○ Frustrated
○ Sad   ○ Anxious
○ Content   ○ Tired
○ Overwhelmed ○ Bored
○ Insecure   ○ Sick
○ Excited   ○ Angry
○ Lonely   ○ Emotionless
○ _____

I am brave.
I am kind.
I am smart.
I am loved.
I am beautiful.
I am capable.
I am confident.

RATE YOUR OVERALL WELLNESS

😊 😐 😯 ☹️ 😢 😶 😑

DATE _____

M T **W** T **F** S **S**

WATER
○ ○ ○ ○ ○ ○ ○ ○ ○ ○

MY SLEEP LAST NIGHT WAS...
😍 Great 😊 Good 😐 Okay 😟 Not good 😫 Awful

gratitude
What am I grateful for today?

self-reflect
Actions, reactions & positive change.

What do I need to take care of myself today?
_____
_____
_____
_____

What have I learned about myself lately?
_____
_____
_____
_____

How can I be kinder to myself today?
_____
_____
_____
_____
_____
_____
_____

mindfulness
What thoughts & emotions have been on my mind?

self-care
Are you finding balance?

Think about each of the life categories to the right.

Rate each category from 1 - 10.

Wheel of life: PERSONAL GROWTH, HEALTH, FRIENDS, RELATIONSHIPS, RECREATION, SPIRITUALITY, CAREER, FINANCE — scale 1 to 10

self-aware
How am I today?

○ Happy   ○ Frustrated
○ Sad   ○ Anxious
○ Content   ○ Tired
○ Overwhelmed   ○ Bored
○ Insecure   ○ Sick
○ Excited   ○ Angry
○ Lonely   ○ Emotionless
○ _____

RATE YOUR OVERALL WELLNESS

DATE _____

M T W T F S S

WATER
◊ ◊ ◊ ◊ ◊ ◊ ◊ ◊

MY SLEEP LAST NIGHT WAS...
Great Good Okay Not good Awful

gratitude
What am I grateful for today?

self-reflect
Actions, reactions & positive change.

What do I need to take care of myself today?
_____
_____
_____

What have I learned about myself lately?
_____
_____
_____
_____

mindfulness
What thoughts & emotions have been on my mind?

How can I be kinder to myself today?
_____
_____
_____
_____
_____
_____

self-care
Are you finding balance?

Think about each of the life categories to the right.

Rate each category from 1 - 10.

PERSONAL GROWTH · HEALTH · FRIENDS · RELATIONSHIPS · RECREATION · SPIRITUALITY · CAREER · FINANCE

1 2 3 4 5 6 7 8 9 10

self-aware
How am I today?

○ Happy   ○ Frustrated
○ Sad   ○ Anxious
○ Content   ○ Tired
○ Overwhelmed   ○ Bored
○ Insecure   ○ Sick
○ Excited   ○ Angry
○ Lonely   ○ Emotionless
○ _____

RATE YOUR OVERALL WELLNESS

DATE _____

M T **W** T **F** S **S**

WATER
○ ○ ○ ○ ○ ○ ○ ○ ○ ○

MY SLEEP LAST NIGHT WAS...
😍 Great 🙂 Good 😐 Okay 🙁 Not good 😣 Awful

gratitude
What am I grateful for today?

self-reflect
Actions, reactions & positive change.

What do I need to take care of myself today?
_____
_____
_____

What have I learned about myself lately?
_____
_____
_____

mindfulness
What thoughts & emotions have been on my mind?

How can I be kinder to myself today?
_____
_____
_____
_____
_____

self-care
Are you finding balance?

Think about each of the life categories to the right.

Rate each category from 1 - 10.

Wheel categories: PERSONAL GROWTH, HEALTH, FRIENDS, RELATIONSHIPS, RECREATION, SPIRITUALITY, CAREER, FINANCE

self-aware
How am I today?

○ Happy   ○ Frustrated
○ Sad   ○ Anxious
○ Content   ○ Tired
○ Overwhelmed   ○ Bored
○ Insecure   ○ Sick
○ Excited   ○ Angry
○ Lonely   ○ Emotionless
○ _____

RATE YOUR OVERALL WELLNESS	DATE
😊 😐 😮 😠 😢 😀 😑	M T W T F S S

WATER
💧 💧 💧 💧 💧 💧 💧 💧

MY SLEEP LAST NIGHT WAS...
😍 Great 😊 Good 😐 Okay 😟 Not good 😣 Awful

gratitude
What am I grateful for today?

self-reflect
Actions, reactions & positive change.

What do I need to take care of myself today?
_____
_____
_____

What have I learned about myself lately?
_____
_____
_____

mindfulness
What thoughts & emotions have been on my mind?

How can I be kinder to myself today?
_____
_____
_____
_____
_____

self-care

Are you finding balance?

Think about each of the life categories to the right.

Rate each category from 1 - 10.

Wheel of life categories: PERSONAL GROWTH, HEALTH, FINANCE, FRIENDS, CAREER, RELATIONSHIPS, SPIRITUALITY, RECREATION (1-10 scale)

self-aware
How am I today?

- ○ Happy
- ○ Sad
- ○ Content
- ○ Overwhelmed
- ○ Insecure
- ○ Excited
- ○ Lonely
- ○ _____

- ○ Frustrated
- ○ Anxious
- ○ Tired
- ○ Bored
- ○ Sick
- ○ Angry
- ○ Emotionless

RATE YOUR OVERALL WELLNESS	DATE
😊 😌 😶 😠 😢 😐 🙂	**M** T **W** T **F** S **S**

WATER 💧💧💧💧💧💧💧💧

MY SLEEP LAST NIGHT WAS...
😍 Great 😊 Good 😐 Okay 😟 Not good 😢 Awful

gratitude
What am I grateful for today?

self-reflect
Actions, reactions & positive change.

What do I need to take care of myself today?
_____
_____
_____

What have I learned about myself lately?
_____
_____
_____

mindfulness
What thoughts & emotions have been on my mind?

How can I be kinder to myself today?
_____
_____
_____
_____
_____

self-care

Are you finding balance?

Think about each of the life categories to the right.

Rate each category from 1 - 10.

Wheel of life chart with categories: PERSONAL GROWTH, HEALTH, FRIENDS, RELATIONSHIPS, RECREATION, SPIRITUALITY, CAREER, FINANCE (scale 1-10)

self-aware
How am I today?

- ○ Happy
- ○ Sad
- ○ Content
- ○ Overwhelmed
- ○ Insecure
- ○ Excited
- ○ Lonely
- ○ _____

- ○ Frustrated
- ○ Anxious
- ○ Tired
- ○ Bored
- ○ Sick
- ○ Angry
- ○ Emotionless

RATE YOUR OVERALL WELLNESS	DATE
🙂 😐 😶 😠 😢 😊 😑	M T W T F S S

WATER 💧💧💧💧💧💧💧💧💧

MY SLEEP LAST NIGHT WAS...
😍 Great 🙂 Good 😐 Okay 😟 Not good 😣 Awful

gratitude
What am I grateful for today?

self-reflect
Actions, reactions & positive change.

What do I need to take care of myself today?
_____
_____
_____

What have I learned about myself lately?
_____
_____
_____

mindfulness
What thoughts & emotions have been on my mind?

How can I be kinder to myself today?
_____
_____
_____
_____
_____

self-care
Are you finding balance?

Think about each of the life categories to the right.

Rate each category from 1 - 10.

Wheel of life diagram with categories: PERSONAL GROWTH, HEALTH, FRIENDS, RELATIONSHIPS, RECREATION, SPIRITUALITY, CAREER, FINANCE (scale 1-10)

self-aware
How am I today?

○ Happy   ○ Frustrated
○ Sad   ○ Anxious
○ Content   ○ Tired
○ Overwhelmed   ○ Bored
○ Insecure   ○ Sick
○ Excited   ○ Angry
○ Lonely   ○ Emotionless
○ _____

RATE YOUR OVERALL WELLNESS	DATE
😊 😐 😶 😠 😢 😶‍🌫️ 😑	M T W T F S S

WATER
💧 💧 💧 💧 💧 💧 💧 💧

MY SLEEP LAST NIGHT WAS...
😍 Great 🙂 Good 😐 Okay 😟 Not good 😣 Awful

gratitude
What am I grateful for today?

self-reflect
Actions, reactions & positive change.

What do I need to take care of myself today?
_____
_____
_____
_____

What have I learned about myself lately?
_____
_____
_____
_____

How can I be kinder to myself today?
_____
_____
_____
_____
_____
_____
_____

mindfulness
What thoughts & emotions have been on my mind?

self-care

Are you finding balance?

Think about each of the life categories to the right.

Rate each category from 1 - 10.

Wheel with categories: PERSONAL GROWTH, HEALTH, FRIENDS, RELATIONSHIPS, RECREATION, SPIRITUALITY, CAREER, FINANCE (scale 1-10)

self-aware
How am I today?

- ○ Happy
- ○ Sad
- ○ Content
- ○ Overwhelmed
- ○ Insecure
- ○ Excited
- ○ Lonely
- ○ _____

- ○ Frustrated
- ○ Anxious
- ○ Tired
- ○ Bored
- ○ Sick
- ○ Angry
- ○ Emotionless

RATE YOUR OVERALL WELLNESS

DATE _____

M T W T F S S

WATER
◊ ◊ ◊ ◊ ◊ ◊ ◊ ◊

MY SLEEP LAST NIGHT WAS...
Great Good Okay Not good Awful

gratitude
What am I grateful for today?

self-reflect
Actions, reactions & positive change.

What do I need to take care of myself today?
_____
_____
_____
_____

What have I learned about myself lately?
_____
_____
_____
_____
_____

mindfulness
What thoughts & emotions have been on my mind?

How can I be kinder to myself today?
_____
_____
_____
_____
_____
_____

self-care

Are you finding balance?

Think about each of the life categories to the right.

Rate each category from 1 - 10.

PERSONAL GROWTH · HEALTH · FRIENDS · RELATIONSHIPS · RECREATION · SPIRITUALITY · CAREER · FINANCE

1 2 3 4 5 6 7 8 9 10

self-aware
How am I today?

○ Happy   ○ Frustrated
○ Sad   ○ Anxious
○ Content   ○ Tired
○ Overwhelmed ○ Bored
○ Insecure   ○ Sick
○ Excited   ○ Angry
○ Lonely   ○ Emotionless
○ _____

RATE YOUR OVERALL WELLNESS	DATE _____
😊 😌 😮 😠 😢 😬 😐	**M** T **W** T **F** S **S**

WATER
💧 💧 💧 💧 💧 💧 💧 💧

MY SLEEP LAST NIGHT WAS...
😍 Great 😊 Good 😐 Okay 😟 Not good 😣 Awful

gratitude
What am I grateful for today?

self-reflect
Actions, reactions & positive change.

What do I need to take care of myself today?
_____
_____
_____
_____

What have I learned about myself lately?
_____
_____
_____
_____

mindfulness
What thoughts & emotions have been on my mind?

How can I be kinder to myself today?
_____
_____
_____
_____
_____
_____
_____

self-care

Are you finding balance?

Think about each of the life categories to the right.

Rate each category from 1 - 10.

(Wheel with categories: PERSONAL GROWTH, HEALTH, FRIENDS, RELATIONSHIPS, RECREATION, SPIRITUALITY, CAREER, FINANCE — rated 1-10)

self-aware
How am I today?

- ○ Happy
- ○ Sad
- ○ Content
- ○ Overwhelmed
- ○ Insecure
- ○ Excited
- ○ Lonely
- ○ _____

- ○ Frustrated
- ○ Anxious
- ○ Tired
- ○ Bored
- ○ Sick
- ○ Angry
- ○ Emotionless

RATE YOUR OVERALL WELLNESS

😊 🙁 😮 😣 😢 😶 😐

DATE _____

[M] T [W] T [F] s [S]

WATER

💧 💧 💧 💧 💧 💧 💧 💧 💧 💧

MY SLEEP LAST NIGHT WAS...

😍 Great 🙂 Good 😐 Okay 😕 Not good 😣 Awful

gratitude
What am I grateful for today?

self-reflect
Actions, reactions & positive change.

What do I need to take care of myself today?
_____
_____
_____
_____

What have I learned about myself lately?
_____
_____
_____
_____

mindfulness
What thoughts & emotions have been on my mind?

How can I be kinder to myself today?
_____
_____
_____
_____
_____
_____
_____

self-care

Are you finding balance?

Think about each of the life categories to the right.

Rate each category from 1 - 10.

PERSONAL GROWTH · HEALTH · FRIENDS · RELATIONSHIPS · RECREATION · SPIRITUALITY · CAREER · FINANCE

1 2 3 4 5 6 7 8 9 10

self-aware
How am I today?

○ Happy ○ Frustrated
○ Sad ○ Anxious
○ Content ○ Tired
○ Overwhelmed ○ Bored
○ Insecure ○ Sick
○ Excited ○ Angry
○ Lonely ○ Emotionless
○ _____

RATE YOUR OVERALL WELLNESS	DATE
😊 🙂 😐 😠 😢 😶 🙃	M T W T F S S

WATER
💧 💧 💧 💧 💧 💧 💧 💧

MY SLEEP LAST NIGHT WAS...
😴 Great 🙂 Good 😐 Okay 😟 Not good 😩 Awful

gratitude
What am I grateful for today?

self-reflect
Actions, reactions & positive change.

What do I need to take care of myself today?
_____
_____
_____

What have I learned about myself lately?
_____
_____
_____

mindfulness
What thoughts & emotions have been on my mind?

How can I be kinder to myself today?
_____
_____
_____
_____
_____

self-care

Are you finding balance?

Think about each of the life categories to the right.

Rate each category from 1 - 10.

Wheel categories: PERSONAL GROWTH, HEALTH, FRIENDS, RELATIONSHIPS, RECREATION, SPIRITUALITY, CAREER, FINANCE
Scale: 1 2 3 4 5 6 7 8 9 10

self-aware
How am I today?

- ○ Happy
- ○ Sad
- ○ Content
- ○ Overwhelmed
- ○ Insecure
- ○ Excited
- ○ Lonely
- ○ _____

- ○ Frustrated
- ○ Anxious
- ○ Tired
- ○ Bored
- ○ Sick
- ○ Angry
- ○ Emotionless

Be kind to yourself.

GUIDED PROMPT

DATE _____

GRATITUDE

EXCERCICSE

List 3 things you are grateful for today.

_____
_____
_____
_____
_____

AFFIRMATION

Be your own hype person. Craft a concise affirmation to reinforce your innate strength, unique qualities, and unwavering power.

CREATIVE VISUALIZATION

Draw a picture that represents gratitude.
(ex. a smile, a sunrise, the feeling of being thankful.)

GUIDED PROMPT DATE _____

MINDFULNESS

EXCERCICSE

Practice a 5-minute breathing exercise. Write down how you feel before & immediately after.

AFFIRMATION

Be your own hype person. Craft a concise affirmation to reinforce your innate strength, unique qualities, and unwavering power.

CREATIVE VISUALIZATION

Draw a picture of how you felt before and after your 5-minute breathing excercise.

GUIDED PROMPT

DATE _____

POSITIVE THINKING

EXCERCICSE

Find a silver lining in a challenging situation you recently experienced. Describe below.

```
_____
_____
_____
_____
_____
_____
```

AFFIRMATION

Be your own hype person. Craft a concise affirmation to reinforce your innate strength, unique qualities, and unwavering power.

CREATIVE VISUALIZATION

Draw a picture that represents a silver lining. (ex. the sun setting but then rising again.)

GUIDED PROMPT   DATE _____

SELF-REFLECTION

EXCERCICSE

Write about a core value that guides your decisions.

AFFIRMATION

Be your own hype person. Craft a concise affirmation to reinforce your innate strength, unique qualities, and unwavering power.

CREATIVE VISUALIZATION

Draw a picture representing guidence. (ex. an older sibling, a compass, a teacher)

GUIDED PROMPT

DATE _____

GRATITUDE

EXCERCICSE

Write a thank you note to someone who has helped you - can be recently or in the past.

AFFIRMATION

Be your own hype person. Craft a concise affirmation to reinforce your innate strength, unique qualities, and unwavering power.

CREATIVE VISUALIZATION

Draw a picture representing support & love for others.
(ex. hands reaching out or a hug)

GUIDED PROMPT   DATE _____

MINDFULNESS

EXCERCICSE

Practice a grounding technique [uses the 5 senses to help you move through distress] & describe how it felt. (ex. holding ice or putting hands in water.)

_____
_____
_____
_____
_____
_____

AFFIRMATION

Be your own hype person. Craft a concise affirmation to reinforce your innate strength, unique qualities, and unwavering power.

CREATIVE VISUALIZATION

Draw a picture representing the feeling you experience when you are overwhelmed.

GUIDED PROMPT DATE _____

POSITIVE THINKING

EXCERCICSE

List 5 things you like about yourself.

```
_____

_____

_____

_____

_____
```

AFFIRMATION

Be your own hype person. Craft a concise affirmation to reinforce your innate strength, unique qualities, and unwavering power.

CREATIVE VISUALIZATION

Draw a picture representing something you like about yourself.

| GUIDED PROMPT | DATE _____ |

SELF-REFLECTION

EXCERCICSE

Reflect on how you have grown in the past year.

AFFIRMATION

Be your own hype person. Craft a concise affirmation to reinforce your innate strength, unique qualities, and unwavering power.

CREATIVE VISUALIZATION

Draw a picture representing growth.

GUIDED PROMPT

DATE _____

GRATITUDE

EXCERCICSE

Write down something positive that happened today. Can be a simple as just waking up!

AFFIRMATION

Be your own hype person. Craft a concise affirmation to reinforce your innate strength, unique qualities, and unwavering power.

CREATIVE VISUALIZATION

Draw a picture representing how your positive experience made you feel.

GUIDED PROMPT DATE _____

MINDFULNESS

EXCERCICSE

Describe a sensory experience you enjoyed today. [An experience that connects w/the 5 senses] (ex. the smell of the ocean reminds you of vacation.)

AFFIRMATION

Be your own hype person. Craft a concise affirmation to reinforce your innate strength, unique qualities, and unwavering power.

CREATIVE VISUALIZATION

Draw a picture that represents joy.

GUIDED PROMPT   DATE _____

POSITIVE THINKING

EXCERCICSE

Identify a negative thought and replace it with a positive one. Describe below.

```
_____
_____
_____
_____
_____
_____
```

AFFIRMATION

Be your own hype person. Craft a concise affirmation to reinforce your innate strength, unique qualities, and unwavering power.

CREATIVE VISUALIZATION

Draw a picture representing the positive thought you used to replace the negative one.

GUIDED PROMPT DATE _____

SELF-REFLECTION

EXCERCICSE

Write about a lesson you learned from a past mistake.

AFFIRMATION

Be your own hype person. Craft a concise affirmation to reinforce your innate strength, unique qualities, and unwavering power.

CREATIVE VISUALIZATION

Draw a picture that represents growth.

GUIDED PROMPT DATE _____

GRATITUDE

EXCERCICSE

Describe a moment of kindness you experienced or witnessed - recently or in the past.

AFFIRMATION

Be your own hype person. Craft a concise affirmation to reinforce your innate strength, unique qualities, and unwavering power.

CREATIVE VISUALIZATION

Draw a picture that represents kindness.

GUIDED PROMPT   DATE _____

MINDFULNESS

EXCERCICSE

List 3 ways you can practice self-care this week.

```
_____

_____

_____

_____

_____
```

AFFIRMATION

Be your own hype person. Craft a concise affirmation to reinforce your innate strength, unique qualities, and unwavering power.

CREATIVE VISUALIZATION

Draw a picture representing self-care.

GUIDED PROMPT   DATE _____

POSITIVE THINKING

EXCERCICSE

Identify and challenge a limiting belief you've recently had.

```
_____
_____
_____
_____
_____
_____
```

AFFIRMATION

Be your own hype person. Craft a concise affirmation to reinforce your innate strength, unique qualities, and unwavering power.

CREATIVE VISUALIZATION

Draw a picture representing a challenging situation.

GUIDED PROMPT DATE _____

SELF-REFLECTION

EXCERCICSE

Write about a time you overcame a challenge.

_____
_____
_____
_____
_____
_____

AFFIRMATION

Be your own hype person. Craft a concise affirmation to reinforce your innate strength, unique qualities, and unwavering power.

CREATIVE VISUALIZATION

Draw a picture that represents overcoming a challenge.

GUIDED PROMPT   DATE _____

GRATITUDE

EXCERCICSE

Name a person who has inspired you and why.

```
┌─────────────────────────────────────────┐
│  _____  │
│                                         │
│  _____  │
│                                         │
│  _____  │
│                                         │
│  _____  │
│                                         │
│  _____  │
│                                         │
│  _____  │
└─────────────────────────────────────────┘
```

AFFIRMATION

Be your own hype person. Craft a concise affirmation to reinforce your innate strength, unique qualities, and unwavering power.

CREATIVE VISUALIZATION

Draw a picture representing inspiration.

GUIDED PROMPT DATE _____

MINDFULNESS

EXCERCICSE

Take a walk or simply sit outside. Focus on the sounds and sights around you. What did you hear, feel, see?

AFFIRMATION

Be your own hype person. Craft a concise affirmation to reinforce your innate strength, unique qualities, and unwavering power.

CREATIVE VISUALIZATION

Draw a picture representing what you heard, felt, saw.

GUIDED PROMPT   DATE _____

POSITIVE THINKING

EXCERCICSE

Write a letter to your future self, offering encouragement.

AFFIRMATION

Be your own hype person. Craft a concise affirmation to reinforce your innate strength, unique qualities, and unwavering power.

CREATIVE VISUALIZATION

Draw a picture representing your future self.

GUIDED PROMPT　　　　　　　　　　DATE _____

SELF-REFLECTION

EXCERCICSE

Think about a personal strength and how you can use it.

```
_____
_____
_____
_____
_____
_____
```

AFFIRMATION

Be your own hype person. Craft a concise affirmation to reinforce your innate strength, unique qualities, and unwavering power.

CREATIVE VISUALIZATION

Draw a picture representing strength.

GUIDED PROMPT

DATE _____

SELF-REFLECTION

EXCERCICSE

Describe a recent interaction that brought you joy.

```
┌─────────────────────────────────────────┐
│  _____    │
│                                         │
│  _____    │
│                                         │
│  _____    │
│                                         │
│  _____    │
│                                         │
│  _____    │
│                                         │
│  _____    │
└─────────────────────────────────────────┘
```

AFFIRMATION

Be your own hype person. Craft a concise affirmation to reinforce your innate strength, unique qualities, and unwavering power.

CREATIVE VISUALIZATION

Draw a picture representing this joyful interaction.

GUIDED PROMPT   DATE _____

MINDFULNESS

EXCERCICSE

Think about your last meal. What did you like and dislike about it? How did it make you feel? Describe below.

AFFIRMATION

Be your own hype person. Craft a concise affirmation to reinforce your innate strength, unique qualities, and unwavering power.

CREATIVE VISUALIZATION

Draw a picture of the emotions you experienced during your most recent meal.

GUIDED PROMPT   DATE _____

POSITIVE THINKING

EXCERCICSE

Envision your ideal day and describe it.

AFFIRMATION

Be your own hype person. Craft a concise affirmation to reinforce your innate strength, unique qualities, and unwavering power.

CREATIVE VISUALIZATION

Draw a picture representing your ideal day.

| GUIDED PROMPT | DATE _____ |

SELF-REFLECTION

EXCERCICSE

Write about a recent accomplishment and how it felt.

```
_____
_____
_____
_____
_____
_____
```

AFFIRMATION

Be your own hype person. Craft a concise affirmation to reinforce your innate strength, unique qualities, and unwavering power.

CREATIVE VISUALIZATION

Draw a picture representing your accomplishment.

GUIDED PROMPT   DATE _____

GRATITUDE

EXCERCICSE

List 3 people who have supported you and why - can be recently or in the past.

```
_____

_____

_____

_____

_____
```

AFFIRMATION

Be your own hype person. Craft a concise affirmation to reinforce your innate strength, unique qualities, and unwavering power.

CREATIVE VISUALIZATION

Draw a picture representing how you feel when supported.

GUIDED PROMPT DATE _____

MINDFULNESS

EXCERCICSE

Try a 10-minute body scan meditation, starting from your toes & moving up to your head. Write down your thoughts as you scan through your body.

AFFIRMATION

Be your own hype person. Craft a concise affirmation to reinforce your innate strength, unique qualities, and unwavering power.

CREATIVE VISUALIZATION

Draw a picture representing how you feel about your body.

GUIDED PROMPT

DATE _____

POSITIVE THINKING

EXCERCICSE

Write about a personal goal and how you will achieve it.

AFFIRMATION

Be your own hype person. Craft a concise affirmation to reinforce your innate strength, unique qualities, and unwavering power.

CREATIVE VISUALIZATION

Draw a picture representing your goal.

GUIDED PROMPT DATE _____

SELF-REFLECTION

EXCERCICSE

Write about a time you showed courage.

AFFIRMATION

Be your own hype person. Craft a concise affirmation to reinforce your innate strength, unique qualities, and unwavering power.

CREATIVE VISUALIZATION

Draw a picture representing courage.

GUIDED PROMPT

DATE _____

GRATITUDE

EXCERCICSE

List 3 experiences that made you feel alive - can be recently or in the past.

AFFIRMATION

Be your own hype person. Craft a concise affirmation to reinforce your innate strength, unique qualities, and unwavering power.

CREATIVE VISUALIZATION

Draw a picture representing life.

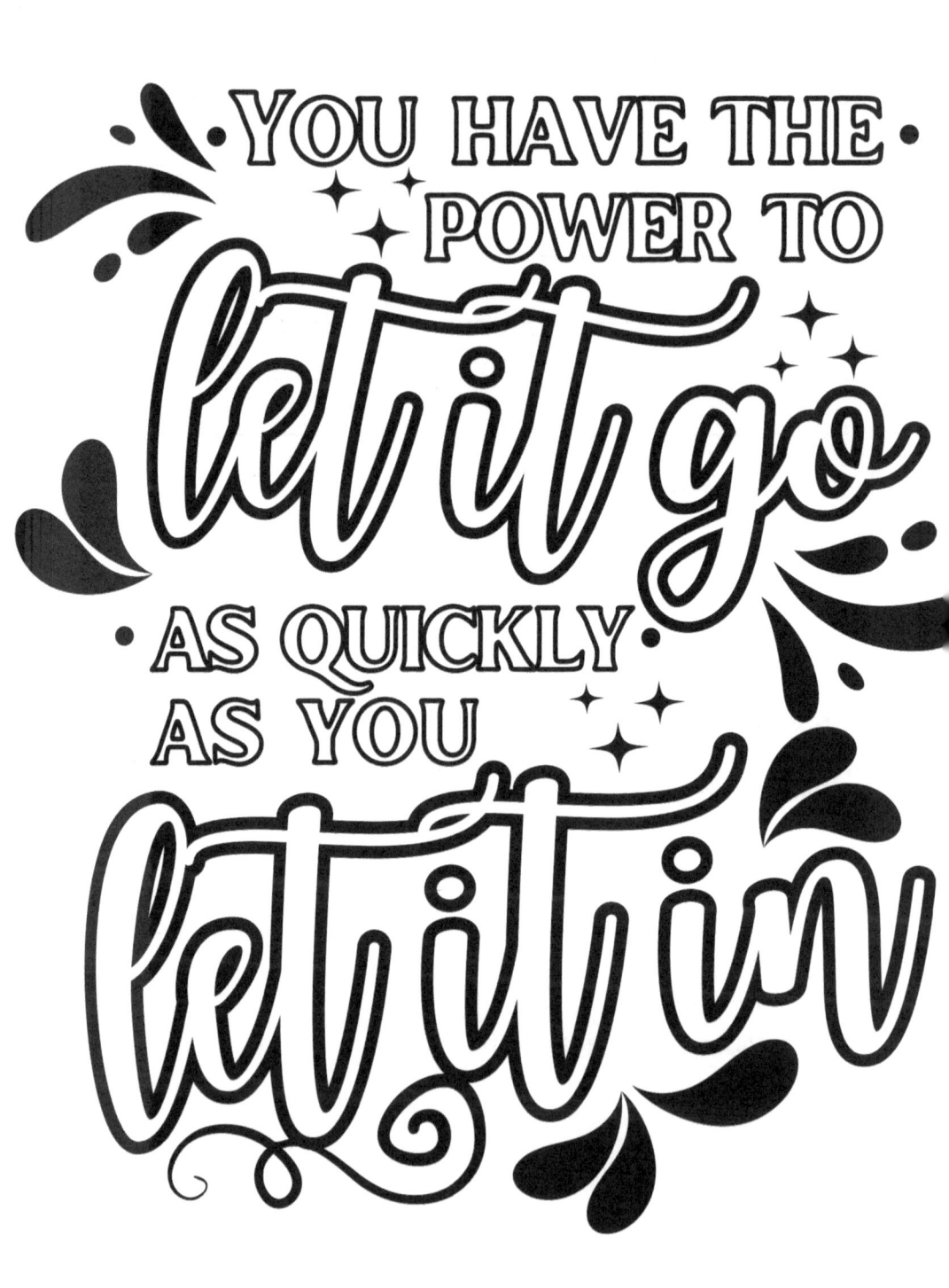

YOU HAVE THE POWER TO *let it go* AS QUICKLY AS YOU *let it in*

5 MINUTE JOURNALING

DATE _____

5 MINUTE JOURNALING

DATE _____

5 MINUTE JOURNALING

DATE _____

5 MINUTE JOURNALING

DATE _____

5 MINUTE JOURNALING

DATE _____

5 MINUTE JOURNALING

DATE _____

5 MINUTE JOURNALING

DATE _____

5 MINUTE JOURNALING

DATE _____

5 MINUTE JOURNALING

DATE _____

5 MINUTE JOURNALING

DATE _____

5 MINUTE JOURNALING

DATE _____

5 MINUTE JOURNALING

DATE _____

5 MINUTE JOURNALING

DATE _____

5 MINUTE JOURNALING

DATE _____

5 MINUTE JOURNALING

DATE _____

5 MINUTE JOURNALING

DATE _____

5 MINUTE JOURNALING

DATE _____

5 MINUTE JOURNALING

DATE _____

5 MINUTE JOURNALING

DATE _____

5 MINUTE JOURNALING

DATE _____

This isn't the end, it's just the beginning.

Made in United States
Troutdale, OR
09/10/2023